MW01613524

WHAT DRIVES WINNING TEAMS

BY BRETT LEDBETTER

Printed in the United States of America

Books may be purchased in quantity and/or special sales by contacting What Drives Winning at info@whatdriveswinning.com or visiting WhatDrivesWinning.com.

Library of Congress In-Publication data has been applied for.

ISBN: 978-0-9962264-2-4

Cover and interior design by Lisa Kuntz

FIRST EDITION

10 9 8 7 6 5 4 3 2 1

THE IDEAS IN THIS BOOK INSPIRED THE
WHAT DRIVES WINNING TEAMS DOCUSERIES
FILMED AT THE 2019 CONFERENCE

——— LEARN MORE ———
Teams.WhatDrivesWinning.com

TABLE OF CONTENTS

A Special Thank You:
To all the people who have shared their thoughts and helped shape my thinking around this book.

WHAT
DRIVES
WINNING
TEAMS

PART 1

STRIVING FOR GROWTH

Reflect on how you would
answer the following two questions. 〉

Two Questions

1.) What are the top three things that could get in the way of your team maximizing its ability?

2.) What's your biggest personal struggle that not many people know about?

WHAT GETS IN THE WAY

WHAT GETS IN THE WAY

Anytime I start working with a team, I begin by asking two questions.

1.) What are the top three things that could get in the way of your team maximizing its ability? (The only thing I ask them to leave off the list is injury because it's largely out of their control.)

2.) What's your biggest personal struggle that not many people know about?

I give them a sheet of paper that looks like this:

I ask them for their best energy, because their honesty is critical for the exercise to be effective.

As soon as everyone is done writing down their answers, we fold the sheet of paper in half to separate the team issues from the individual issues.

The bottom half of the handout is aimed at personal struggles. I've found that it's important to know the personal struggles of the people you're working with because it can give you context about where they are—especially if it feels like they're hard to reach.

When I've asked athletes to write down their answers, here are some of the responses they've given:

"My dad puts so much pressure on me. I feel like how I play is directly tied to his happiness level."

"I feel like I'm responsible for my family's financial future."

"I have a strong desire to please everyone all the time. I care too much about what people think about me."

"My best friend and cousin were murdered."

"I'm afraid to make mistakes in the game. I forget by risking nothing, I'm risking everything."

"I'm dealing with family members' addictions. I'm afraid it might happen to me."

"I don't know what I'm going to do with my life. I'm constantly worried about the future."

"I'm never satisfied. I feel like I'm always pushing instead of being content. I'm always trying to fix things according to my plan, instead of listening and being open-minded to others' thoughts and ways."

"I don't like who or what I see in the mirror."

As you can see, everyone is dealing with something, and these personal struggles are great conversation starters to build relationships. The purpose of the question is to help figure out what's going on—on the inside.

Here are some of the most common themes that I see:

PERSONAL STRUGGLES

MOST COMMON ANSWERS

Confidence	Body Image/Appearance	Following/Trusting God's Plan
Family Issues	Not Being Present	Sense of Belonging
Caring About What Others Think	Work/Life Balance	Comparing Myself to Others
Communication	Hard on Myself	Indecisiveness/Overthinking
Fear of Failure	Perfectionism	Independence
Being Trustwilling	Courage	Injury/Recovery
Anxiety	Being Away from Home	Not Being Wanted
Time Management	School	Physical Health
Not Meeting Expectations	Disorders (OCD, Bipolar, etc.)	Financial Troubles
Depression	Negative Thinking	Focus

Think about yourself. Think about your team. Can you relate?

We don't always talk about the personal struggles in a team setting, especially if someone asks (before writing their answers), "Who's going to read these?" It depends on the trust level within the group.

I usually approach the athlete on an individual basis. Later in the book, I'll show you what that looks like. For now, let's focus on the team.

Let's go back to the top half of the handout.

What are the top three things that could get in the way of your team maximizing its ability?

Here are some of the most common answers that I see:

WHAT GETS IN THE WAY
MOST COMMON ANSWERS

Selfishness	Lack of Common Goal	Lack of Confidence
Social Media	Lack of Accountability	Eating Habits
Lack of Chemistry / Unity	Drama Inside the Team	Academic Demands
Outside Distractions	Poor Internal Leadership	Criticism
Communication Issues	Egos	Lack of Coachability
Negative Attitude	Unhealthy Internal Competition	Partying
Unmotivated	Lack of Discipline	Entitlement
Not Supporting One Another	Lack of Focus	Complacency
Lack of Trust	Third Party Advice	Lack of Buy In
Laziness	Fear of Failure	Expectations

As you look at this list, think about your team. Do you see a lot of these issues inside your locker room?

Here's an example of how I attacked those issues with a basketball team that I worked with.

I had them get into small groups and share their answers about the top three things that could get in the way. I asked them if there were commonalities to their answers.

Once each group had a minute or two to discuss, I asked them to share their answers with the team. Everybody read off all three of their answers.

One player from the team volunteered and wrote down everyone's answers as they called them out.

They tallied any common answers, and once we finished, it looked like this:

Complacency ||
Selfishness ## ## ||||
Lack of Trust ||
Outside Distractions ||
Lack of Buy In |||
Negativity ||
Lack of Effort |||
Self-Doubt ||
Poor Communication
Lack of Focus
Lack of Accountability
Lack of Toughness
Lack of Leadership

What did we create together?

A curriculum of topics (based on what they think is most important) that could take them away from where they wanted to be as a team.

After we finished the list, I asked each player to transfer each answer to a sticky note.

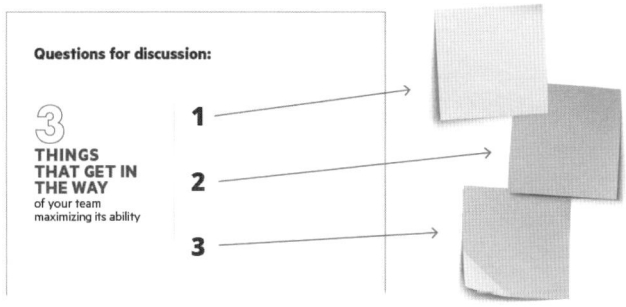

Once they finished, everyone had three sticky notes.

I then drew this on the whiteboard:

HUMAN	SPORT

Then I said, "If your answer is human-related (personal or interpersonal issues), put your sticky note on the left side of the board. If your answer is sport-related (technical or tactical aspects of the sport), put your sticky note on the right side of the board."

So again, here are their answers:

Complacency II
Selfishness ＨＨＴ ＨＨＴ IIII
Lack of Trust II
Outside Distractions II
Lack of Buy In III
Negativity II
Lack of Effort III
Self-Doubt II
Poor Communication
Lack of Focus
Lack of Accountability
Lack of Toughness
Lack of Leadership

Which category are those going to fall under?

Human or Sport?

Every one of the sticky notes went to the human side.

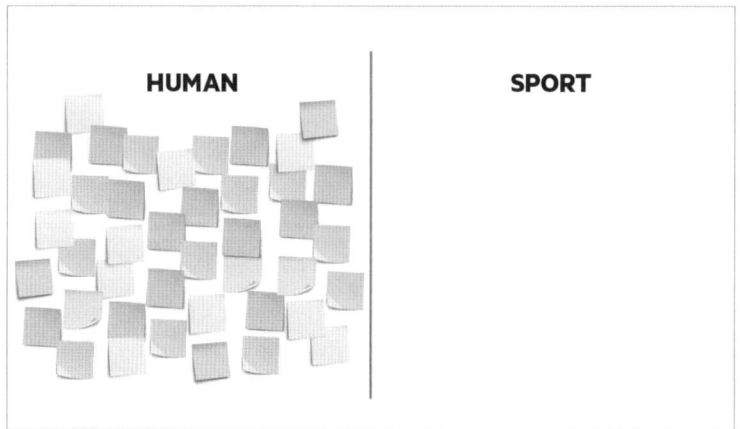

When the players saw that, it created an awareness that these are the bullets that could take the team down.

Of all the teams I've worked with, nearly all boards look like this—it doesn't matter if it's a 5th grade team or a national championship team at the Division I level.

The best teams (and coaches) I've been around, understand that approaching human-related issues is part of the equation that gets results.

Brad Stevens is one of those coaches.

MEET BRAD STEVENS
Brad Stevens has dual citizenship. He's been a successful basketball coach at the college level (Butler Bulldogs), but he's also been successful at the professional level (Boston Celtics).

The two jobs have completely different dynamics in terms of managing the locker room.

Brad broke down his philosophy in each environment. He started with his approach at Butler.

Brad Stevens
Boston Celtics

We're going to try to recruit to our values, which was the foundation of our pyramid, a base of character.

We're going to make sure that we prepare as well as we can, and do that day to day, and not change depending on how we feel, or what happened yesterday, or a winning streak, or a losing streak.

And then we're going to perform as well as we can.

And then the results take care of themselves.

And the point that I was trying to make to our players, is if you focus too much of your time and attention on the results, you're in trouble.

This is what the Butler Pyramid looked like:

Brad liked the pyramid shape because it was a graphic representation of how he invested his energy. As you go up the pyramid, what happens?

Each space gets smaller.

That reflected how Brad prioritized his energy. He spent the most time on the foundational things.

Think back to the sticky notes. Which column were they in? All of the issues fell on the human-related side. Doesn't it make sense why the foundation of the Butler Pyramid would be character?

Brad did say that there was one addition you could make to the pyramid.

Brad Stevens
Boston Celtics

You could probably put a huge base below it that says "Talent," because ultimately you have to have talent to win.

And there's a minimum level of talent to be able to even survive.

But all of those things, when considering equal talent, really add up.

They added up for Brad. He went to back-to-back national championship games. He was the youngest coach in the history of the game to accomplish that. His success led him to an opportunity with the Boston Celtics.

Here are the first four years of Brad's time in Boston:

- 2013-14: 25-57
- 2014-15: 40-42
- 2015-16: 48-34
- 2016-17: 53-29

What do you notice?

Progress...and so did the Celtics.

Which is why, after his third year, he was offered a contract extension. At a press conference following the announcement, he said, *"It's an honor to be a member of the Boston Celtics. We'll continue striving for growth in pursuit of Banner 18."*

Let's take a closer look.

First sentence: *"It's an honor to be a **member** of the Boston Celtics."*

What's the difference between the word *member* and *coach*?

Coach suggests authority. (That doesn't work well going from college to the NBA, where some players have more power than the coach.)

The word *member* suggests that you are a part of something. That speaks to Brad's humility, which is important when coaching powerful professionals.

Let's look at the second sentence.

*"We'll continue **striving for growth** in pursuit of Banner 18."*

I asked him why he said *striving for growth*. Here's what he said.

Brad Stevens
Boston Celtics

Because to me that's what it's all about.

Even if we're fortunate enough to someday achieve that 18th banner for the Celtics, then the next day we're going to be pursuing 19.

So ultimately, it's about getting better.

And you know that's been a fun way to live as a coach, because no matter what, whether you're not having a very good season—you're going through a tough time, or you're really rolling—you're going through a good time, you're just focused on the next day and trying to be a little bit better.

When you focus on growth, that creates emotional consistency. You're not riding the emotional highs and lows that come with outcomes.

That's hard to do in Boston, because of their history.

The Celtics have a blank banner that hangs in the rafters that represents Banner 18, in both the practice facility and in the arena where they play, as a visual reminder of what they're chasing.

There can only be one goal for the Boston Celtics organization: Banner 18.

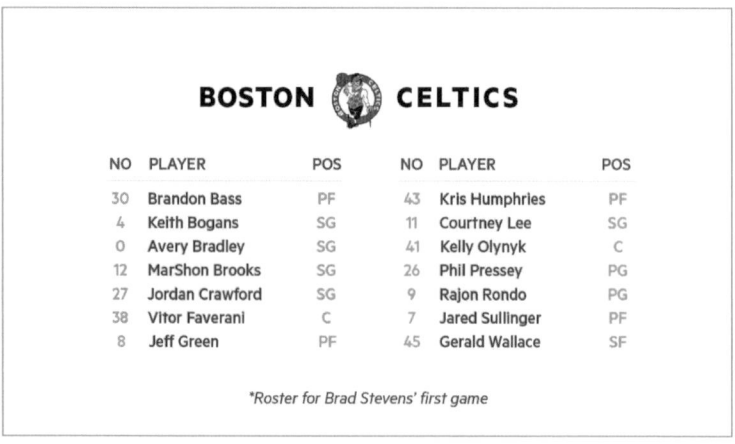

	BOSTON CELTICS 1957 WORLD CHAMPIONS	BOSTON CELTICS 1959 WORLD CHAMPIONS	BOSTON CELTICS 1960 WORLD CHAMPIONS	BOSTON CELTICS 1961 WORLD CHAMPIONS	BOSTON CELTICS 1962 WORLD CHAMPIONS	BOSTON CELTICS 1963 WORLD CHAMPIONS

But, here's what's interesting. Take a look at this roster:

BOSTON CELTICS

NO	PLAYER	POS		NO	PLAYER	POS
30	Brandon Bass	PF		43	Kris Humphries	PF
4	Keith Bogans	SG		11	Courtney Lee	SG
0	Avery Bradley	SG		41	Kelly Olynyk	C
12	MarShon Brooks	SG		26	Phil Pressey	PG
27	Jordan Crawford	SG		9	Rajon Rondo	PG
38	Vitor Faverani	C		7	Jared Sullinger	PF
8	Jeff Green	PF		45	Gerald Wallace	SF

Roster for Brad Stevens' first game

Not one guy from the original roster that Brad took over remains on the team (which speaks to the turnover in the NBA).

Think about this: If the Celtics' goal is Banner 18, a player might not buy into that goal if they're not going to be there in three weeks.

How did Brad create a purpose that everyone can buy into?

Banner 18 may be the goal, but *striving for growth* is the purpose.

That purpose is something everyone can buy into on a daily basis regardless of what happens tomorrow. Why? Because if you grow today, you're better prepared for tomorrow.

The best teams that I've been around are *striving for growth* and it's reflected in their daily process.

WHAT'S THE SOLUTION

WHAT'S THE SOLUTION

How do we strive for growth in the personal realm?

We've worked with a lot of high-level coaches to develop a glossary of character skills that they value most. We created simple, action-oriented definitions for those performance and relational skills.

PERFORMANCE SKILLS

Hardworking: Paying the price with effort

Competitive: Striving to be your best

Positive: Good and useful thinking

Focused: Eliminating distractions

Accountable: Taking responsibility for your actions

Courageous: Operating outside of your comfort zone

Resilient: Bouncing back from setbacks

Confident: Self-trusting

Enthusiastic: Expressing enjoyment

Disciplined: Self-regulating

Motivated: Having a strong purpose

Creative: Out-of-the-box thinking

Curious: Desiring to learn or understand

RELATIONAL SKILLS

Unselfish: Putting the team first

Honest: Telling the truth

Respectful: Showing consideration

Appreciative: Recognizing the good in someone or something

Humble: Distributing credit

Patient: Tolerating delay or struggle

Loyal: Showing allegiance

Trustworthy: Being reliable

Trustwilling: Relying on others

Encouraging: Giving confidence and support

Socially Aware: Understanding signals sent and received

Caring: Investing in the person

Empathetic: Sharing the feelings of others

You can adopt this, or it can serve as a starting point to develop your own program definitions. The key is that everybody on the team operates from the same meaning—that closes the gap of interpretation.

Anytime I work with an individual or a team, I ask them four questions when showing them the glossary.

First Question: If you committed to investing energy into any of these skills, could you improve them? (I've never had an athlete tell me, "No.")

Second Question: Pick three performance skills that you want to improve this upcoming year.

PERFORMANCE SKILLS

Hardworking: Paying the price with effort

Competitive: Striving to be your best

Positive: Good and useful thinking

Focused: Eliminating distractions

Accountable: Taking responsibility for your actions

Courageous: Operating outside of your comfort zone

Resilient: Bouncing back from setbacks

Confident: Self-trusting

Enthusiastic: Expressing enjoyment

Disciplined: Self-regulating

Motivated: Having a strong purpose

Creative: Out-of-the-box thinking

Curious: Desiring to learn or understand

1.)

2.)

3.)

If you got better at those three skills, would that make you a better player? (I've never had an athlete tell me, "No.")

Third Question: Pick three relational skills that you want to improve this upcoming year.

RELATIONAL SKILLS

Unselfish: Putting the team first

Honest: Telling the truth

Respectful: Showing consideration

Appreciative: Recognizing the good in someone or something

Humble: Distributing credit

Patient: Tolerating delay or struggle

Loyal: Showing allegiance

Trustworthy: Being reliable

Trustwilling: Relying on others

Encouraging: Giving confidence and support

Socially Aware: Understanding signals sent and received

Caring: Investing in the person

Empathetic: Sharing the feelings of others

1.)

2.)

3.)

If you got better at those three skills, would that make you a better teammate? (I've never had an athlete tell me, "No.")

Fourth Question: If performance skills make you a better player and relational skills make you a better teammate—do you see how improving those skills would produce better results? (I've never had an athlete tell me, "No.")

With this in mind, why don't more people focus on that?

I'd like to introduce you to someone who does.

MEET JAY WRIGHT

The Villanova men's basketball program has become one of the elite in recent years.

The program is built on one word: ATTITUDE.

Jay Wright, the head coach, gauges a player's attitude by asking one question, "Where is your mindset after something bad happens to you?"

They train their ATTITUDE by creating adverse situations in practice.

That trained response was on full display in 2016 when they played the University of North Carolina for the national championship.

With 13.5 seconds left in the game, North Carolina had the ball, down 74-71.

What do you *not* want to do in this situation if you're Villanova? Give up a three.

Guess what happened? Villanova gave up a three.

Jay Wright explained what happened right before and right after that happened.

Jay Wright
Villanova

We'd blown a 10-point lead. We'd given up a three before that. The only thing you could do wrong on that play was give up a three. We did it.

The guys came off the court, walked to the huddle, and they all said, "Attitude. Attitude." Not one guy complained. Not one guy said, "Do you believe that shot?"

And we were in the huddle and they all just looked at each other like, "This is what we do. Attitude. Attitude. This is what we do."

If it could have ended right there, I would have felt like they had learned the greatest lesson in life.

It didn't end right there, and what happened in the next 4.7 seconds was legendary. (Google "Villanova reactions to Kris Jenkins buzzer beater.")

After Villanova's Kris Jenkins hit the shot to win the game, everyone went nuts. It was pandemonium.

Except for Jay Wright. He stayed calm. Why?

Jay Wright
Villanova

I was feeling a sense of accomplishment already. I was already saying, "If we lose this game in overtime, I don't care.

We're going to use this to teach them for life."

Then Jenkins hit the shot.

I really was like, "Are you kidding me, God? Like we get this too?" You know, that's really what my reaction was.

That huddle was one of Jay's favorite moments in coaching.

Do you know who else was in that huddle? Mikal Bridges.

Mikal's evolution:

True Freshman Year: Redshirted. The coaches explained that they thought it would be best; there was no resistance from Mikal or his family. They bought into the plan.

Redshirt Freshman Year: Sixth man on a national championship team. He embraced his role and did all of the little things.

Sophomore Year: Started. Got better. There was talk of him leaving, but he decided to come back to get his degree.

Junior Year: He took an interest in the development of his teammates and elevated their play on the way to winning his second national championship.

After that year, Mikal decided to go pro and heard the NBA Commissioner, Adam Silver, say, "With the 10th pick in the 2018 NBA Draft, the Philadelphia 76ers select Mikal Bridges, from Villanova University."

His mom, Tyneeha, was excited because she worked for the 76ers, and because Mikal, a Philly kid, dreamed of putting that jersey on. The dream was realized.

And then this happened...

Jay Wright
Villanova

They take him away, he goes in the back to do the interviews. We're still in the green room.

They trade him across the country to Phoenix. He's back in the room doing the media interviews, and they tell him.

Now, he doesn't even get to see his mother.

Finally, half an hour later, we all get back together again.

And he just looked at me and said, "ATTITUDE, coach. This is next play."

That shows how deep the word ATTITUDE runs. Can you imagine having a leader in your locker room with that frame of mind? And what kind of influence he has on everybody else?

Mikal's influence was a big reason that Villanova was nominated for Best Team at the 2018 ESPYS.

WHEN IS IT HARDEST

WHEN IS IT HARDEST

Think about the best leader you know. Pick five characteristics from this glossary that he or she demonstrates on a consistent basis.

PERFORMANCE SKILLS

Hardworking: Paying the price with effort
Competitive: Striving to be your best
Positive: Good and useful thinking
Focused: Eliminating distractions
Accountable: Taking responsibility for your actions
Courageous: Operating outside of your comfort zone
Resilient: Bouncing back from setbacks
Confident: Self-trusting
Enthusiastic: Expressing enjoyment
Disciplined: Self-regulating
Motivated: Having a strong purpose
Creative: Out-of-the-box thinking
Curious: Desiring to learn or understand

RELATIONAL SKILLS

Unselfish: Putting the team first
Honest: Telling the truth
Respectful: Showing consideration
Appreciative: Recognizing the good in someone or something
Humble: Distributing credit
Patient: Tolerating delay or struggle
Loyal: Showing allegiance
Trustworthy: Being reliable
Trustwilling: Relying on others
Encouraging: Giving confidence and support
Socially Aware: Understanding signals sent and received
Caring: Investing in the person
Empathetic: Sharing the feelings of others

That's an exercise I do with athletes to begin the conversation on what earns respect.

The athletes write down the characteristics 1-5 on a sheet of paper.

1. Positive
2. Accountable
3. Honest
4. Creative
5. Encouraging

When they finish, I ask them to draw a line down the middle of the paper to separate the page into two columns.

On the right side, I ask them to make it personal. I ask them to answer this question for each characteristic: "When is it hardest for you to be that?"

They write their answers down.

Here's an example of an athlete that I was working with:

TOP 5	WHEN IS IT HARDEST FOR YOU TO BE...
1. Positive	When I'm surrounded by negativity
2. Accountable	When others are held to a lower standard
3. Honest	When I could lose a friendship/relationship
4. Creative	When I feel micromanaged
5. Encouraging	When the receiver doesn't care/respond

What does the left column show?

It shows me what characteristics the athlete values in a leader.

What does the right column show?

It shows the athlete the space where he or she has to go to earn the respect of their peers: doing the "right" thing when it's the hard thing. When you have the internal strength to be the person you want to be in difficult situations, that generates influence.

Billy Donovan understands that.

MEET BILLY DONOVAN
Billy Donovan won back-to-back national championships at the University of Florida as their head basketball coach.

One of Billy's greatest strengths was his ability to find ways to repurpose difficult situations into opportunities for people to become stronger and move closer toward the person they want to become.

For example, if a player was down, frustrated, or complaining, Billy would ask him in a way he could receive, *"Is that who you want to be?"*

If the answer was "no" (which it almost always was), Billy would ask: *"Then, why are you acting like that?"*

His goal is to try to get the players to take ownership of who they want to be. It's important to understand that Billy is great at picking the right time to ask the right question, in the right way, for each player.

By asking those questions, what's Billy doing? He's giving his players the space to direct themselves as opposed to having the environment dictate their behavior.

Billy knows how to ask those kinds of questions 100 different ways to stimulate self-learning.

He's on that channel because he's seen what happens when his best player has that kind of internal strength.

Joakim Noah was a driving force for the program at the University of Florida. His leadership contributed to back-to-back national championships in 2006 and 2007.

After the team won its first title, *Sports Illustrated* did an article on Joakim. The magazine wanted to put him on the cover.

Think about how most athletes would respond.

Guess what Joakim did?

He said, "Not without my guys." Joakim wasn't going to allow the media to separate him from the team that accomplished the goal together.

This hangs in the Florida offices as the symbol of what an elite teammate looks like:

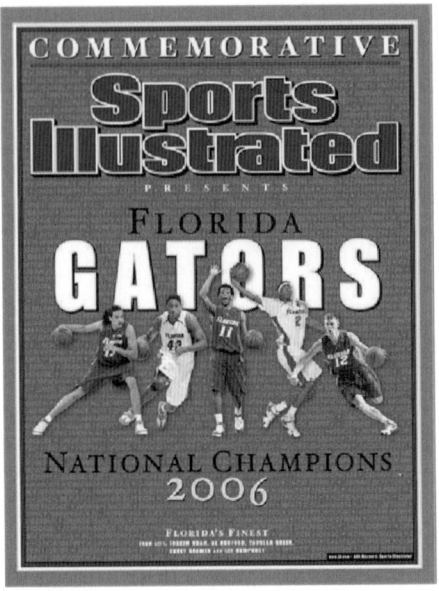

This story gets better.

Almost a decade later, Joakim got a call. He was told, "We want to induct you into the University of Florida Athletic Hall of Fame." Guess what he said?

"Not without my guys."

He wasn't going to be individually recognized for something the group did together.

When you coach a guy like Joakim Noah, that can give you tremendous insight as a coach. Billy reflects on what makes great teams.

Billy Donovan
Oklahoma City Thunder

If I look back on the best teams that I've ever been around, what did those teams have? What was missing from other teams?

Three things:

Love: There was an enormous amount of love inside the team for one another.

Care: There was personal and individual care for each other.

Acceptance: Each and every guy on the team was accepted for who they are.

If you think about that from our own personal lives, if you walked around every single day and said, "I feel loved, I feel accepted, and I feel cared for," our life would be really enriched.

How powerful is that? Contrast love, care, and acceptance with fear, force, and judgement.

Have you ever been on a team where fear, force, and judgement exist?

That's a totally different energy.

When you relentlessly pursue a goal with a group of people who love, care, and accept you for who you are, that's an incredible experience.

THE TAKEAWAY

Think about Brad Stevens. Think about Jay Wright. Think about Billy Donovan. What do they have in common? They're focused on this:

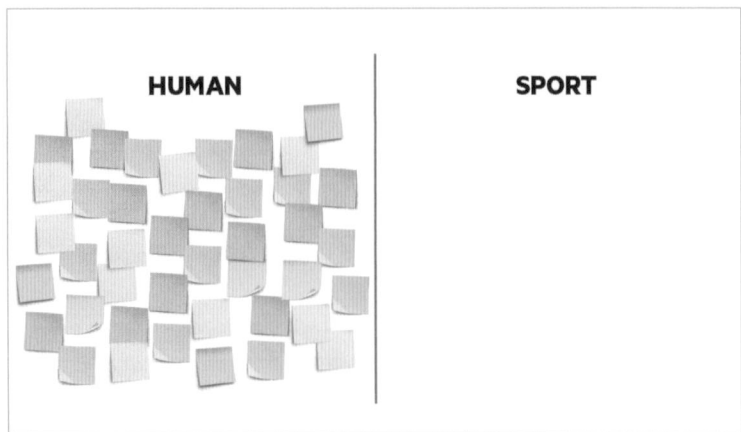

They understand that people drive the process, which drives the results.

In the next two sections, I'm going to show you two different examples of high-performing teams—a men's team and a women's team—who also understand that concept.

Gonzaga Men's Basketball: We're going to look at how they have an organizational approach to create personal growth.

Oregon Women's Basketball: We're going to look at how the best player's personal struggle connected the locker room and led to unprecedented success.

Before I explore Gonzaga, take a look at the next few pages. We've worked with a lot of high-performing athletes, and they shared with us when it's hardest for them to be the characteristics they want to be.

It's hard to deal with something that you haven't detected. The list on the following pages helps build an awareness of the events and situations that take us away from the person we want to be.

One way to use this list: Highlight the bullet points that you can relate to.

The goal: Learn how to repurpose those situations into opportunities to become the person you want to be.

WHEN IS IT HARDEST?

Hardworking: Paying the price with effort
- When I'm not getting the results I want
- When others aren't working hard and getting rewarded
- When it's for someone I don't care about

Competitive: Striving to be your best
- When others around me don't care
- When I feel like I can't win or the goal is out of reach
- When I put my relationship with the person above winning the competition

Positive: Good and useful thinking
- When I'm surrounded by negativity
- When others are overly supportive when I perform poorly
- When supporting something I don't believe in

Focused: Eliminating distractions
- When I don't know how to prioritize things
- When things are too easy
- When others pull my focus elsewhere (friends, family, teammates)

Accountable: Taking responsibility for your actions
- When I don't think I was in the wrong
- When I fear embarrassment/judgment
- When I fear the consequences I'll have to face

Courageous: Operating outside your comfort zone
- When people don't trust me
- When I feel like the risk outweighs the potential reward
- When I fear people won't follow me

Resilient: Bouncing back from setbacks
- When I get knocked down over and over
- When more is asked of me than others
- When the goal seems unattainable

Confident: Self-trusting
- When I overthink
- When I'm not getting results despite full effort
- When I get no reassurance

Enthusiastic: Expressing enjoyment
- If no one responds to it/me
- When I'm too focused on myself
- When I'm surrounded by negative people/energy suckers

Disciplined: Self-regulating
- When no one is watching
- When the wrong choice is easier
- When the result/consequence won't affect me

Motivated: Having a strong purpose
- When I lose sight of my "why"
- When it feels like a lost cause
- When the rewards aren't worth it

Creative: Out-of-the-box thinking
- When authority already has their mind made up
- When I feel micromanaged/controlled
- When my ideas are not valued or are consistently shot down

Curious: Desiring to learn or understand
- When I fear judgment for asking questions
- When I'm scared to know the truth
- When the way I've always done it works

Unselfish: Putting the team first
- When I see others cut corners and get away with it/rewarded for it
- When outside voices are influencing me to be selfish
- When I trust myself more than my teammates

Honest: Telling the truth
- When the truth has negative consequences for me
- When I could lose a friendship/relationship
- When I'm worried what others will think

Respectful: Showing consideration
- When someone gets in the way of what I want
- When someone criticizes me
- When I strongly disagree with someone

Appreciative: Recognizing the good in someone or something
- When I think I deserved it
- When my high-level performance becomes expected
- When someone does me a favor "that comes with a cost"

Humble: Distributing credit
- When outside voices make my head bigger
- When I don't get enough credit
- When I'm the only one performing well

Patient: Tolerating struggle or delay
- When mistakes are effort-based
- When I have to repeat myself
- When something is easy to me and I don't understand others' struggle

Loyal: Showing allegiance
- When friends/family betray me
- When I don't believe in the cause
- When the grass seems greener

Trustworthy: Being reliable
- When it adds unwanted responsibility to me
- When I'm given information that must be shared
- When I'm put in between two people

Trustwilling: Relying on others
- When others have failed me repeatedly
- When my reputation is on the line
- When I don't want to burden others

Encouraging: Giving confidence and support
- When the receiver doesn't care/respond
- When I feel like they didn't earn it
- When I'm jealous of them

Socially Aware: Understanding signals sent and received
- When I'm trying to fit in
- When I'm too focused on myself
- When someone else has different norms

Caring: Investing in the person
- When the person doesn't care for/about themselves
- When I'm overwhelmed with my own issues
- When I'm more invested than they are

Empathetic: Sharing the feelings of others
- When I disagree with their choices/decisions
- When I'm struggling more than they are
- When they ignore clear solutions because it's "too hard"

PART 2

GONZAGA MEN'S BASKETBALL

LOOKING FOR AN ANTI-SPEAKER

Mark Few has been the men's basketball coach at Gonzaga for the last 20 years. His worst year: 23 wins. He's the winningest active coach by percentage at 82%.

Mark and I met in Las Vegas to work on a project together. We explored the idea of me coming to work with his team.

Mark said (as he made a gesture of wringing a towel dry), "We're at like 97%—we're just trying to find a way to make them 2-3% better."

A few weeks later, I got a call from Travis Knight, who has been with Mark for over a decade. He's listed as the head of strength and conditioning, but his role is so much more. In a lot of ways, Travis operates opposite of the industry mindset. He calls his weight room the Dojo (a place where "the way" is taught).

One of Travis's most recent programs is an annual retreat where the team goes to a remote location in the wilderness right before the season starts. In the previous years, they would close the retreat by having a speaker come in and talk with the team. Travis realized it was a great experience, but after a few days, the feeling of excitement slowly wore off.

Gonzaga was looking for something sticky that would leave a lasting impression.

During our conversation, Travis told me that he was looking for an "anti-speaker."

That person would be someone who could facilitate a conversation with the team to help the guys begin the process of finding their voice. This was opposite from the traditional *you speak, we listen* model.

Mark and Travis had identified four objectives as starting points:

- Develop internal leadership
- Deactivate their resistance to growth
- Become response-ready for adversity
- Manage high expectations

FIRST VISIT
PGMs

PGMs

When I met with the team for the first time, I started with the two questions:

1.) What are the top three things that could get in the way of your team maximizing its ability?

2.) What's your biggest personal struggle that not many people know about?

We didn't talk about the personal struggles as a group in the first meeting. Instead, we spent time on the top three things that could get in the way of the team.

They shared their answers in small groups, recorded them on sticky notes, and put them up on the board.

When they finished, their board looked like this:

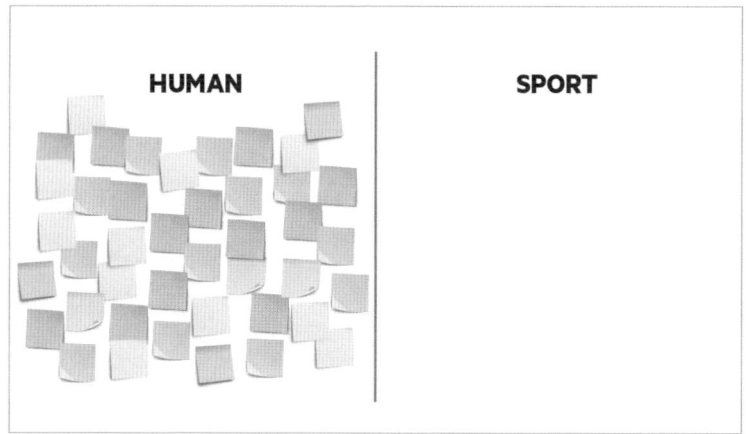

We talked about how Brad Stevens built Butler:

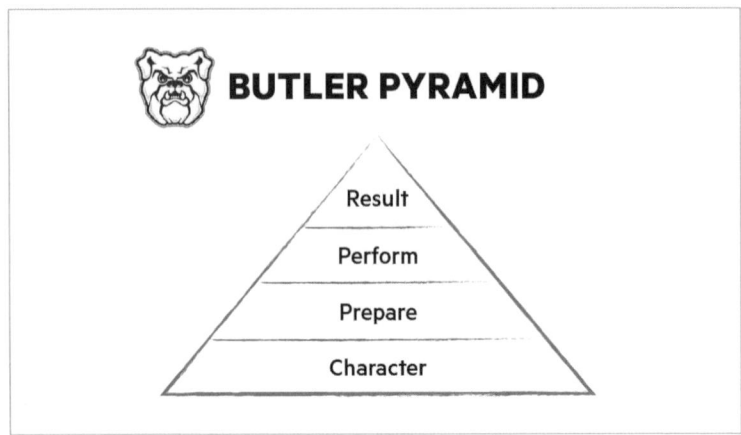

We also talked about how Jay Wright built Villanova:

The Villanova message really struck home because a lot of the players on Gonzaga's current team had played Villanova the previous year. They knew there was something different about that team.

Mark Few said to me, "They out-zagged the Zags."

The message resonated, and momentum was created. Travis and I started to talk about a plan moving forward. We decided that I would come back and meet with the team two more times.

My second visit would be before the conference season, and my third visit would be right before March Madness started. Between my visits, Travis would present what we call PGMs: **P**ersonal **G**rowth **M**ondays.

Every Sunday night, I would talk with Travis. He would give me the context on what had happened, and what would be happening, with the team. I would brainstorm different media assets that he could use to facilitate a discussion.

Once Travis and I had a plan on how the year would run, we presented it to four of the influencers on the team. They loved it. And agreed to move forward with it on one condition: They could start the first PGM with goals.

So that's where we started.

PGM: GOALS

The team came up with five goals:

- ☐ Maui Tournament Championship
- ☐ Regular Season WCC Championship
- ☐ WCC Tournament Championship
- ☐ Top 10 Offensive/Defensive Efficiency
- ☐ National Championship

When I talk to coaches, some are conflicted about setting goals. Why? They're outside of your immediate control, and they're too far down the road.

But when the guys said, "This is what we want to do," Travis and I followed their lead. Travis showed them a video of a Vietnamese schoolboy crossing the road.

As you can see in this picture, the schoolboy is crossing a very busy road.

He does so step by step, and within a few seconds he's lost inside of a sea of cars and scooters as he makes his way to the other side.

After Travis showed it to the team, he asked, "How does this apply to goals?"

They all smiled and shook their heads.

Travis asked, "If you're thinking about lane eight in lane one, what happens?"

Guys started laughing. "You're getting crushed."

The team set a primary goal to "get better every day." That would drive the other goals. The team explored how that happens.

Imagine this circle is your comfort zone.

Your comfort zone in a lot of ways represents your current abilities—things that you're already good at. For you to grow, you have to get outside of your comfort zone.

When you're operating outside your comfort zone, you get into the growth zone. That's where struggle exists. But that's how you stretch your comfort zone.

To incentivize the guys (and to show them how the process works), Travis attached all of their goals to the outside of the growth zone.

As the comfort zone expands, the team grows closer toward their goals. That graphic made a lot of sense to them.

Travis then introduced them to a clip from an interview that I did with Daniel Coyle.

Daniel Coyle wrote a book called *The Talent Code*. His research took him across the world to study talent hotbeds—places that produce statistically impossible results.

One of the questions he investigated: Why are the Japanese kids better than the American kids at math?

One of the reasons we chose that example was because Gonzaga's best player, Rui Hachimura, is from Japan. So anytime we could culturally connect the message to someone on the team, we were going to try and do that. Here's what Coyle found.

Daniel Coyle
"The Talent Code"

There was a great educational study. They were trying to investigate the question of why the Japanese are so much better at math than the U.S. kids.

And they had video cameras in the classroom and taped them for quite a long amount of time. It was an 8th grade algebra class.

It turned out that in the American class, the students were actively struggling, think about the sweet spot here, actively struggling, stretching, reaching, 2% of the time.

In the Japanese class, they were actively struggling 40% of the time.

40% of the time!

In some cases, the teacher would give them the wrong answer so they would struggle more.

They absolutely were honed in on spending more time in the sweet spot, so they learned more.

It's not magic, it's brain science.

After Travis showed the team that clip, he then flashed this up on the screen:

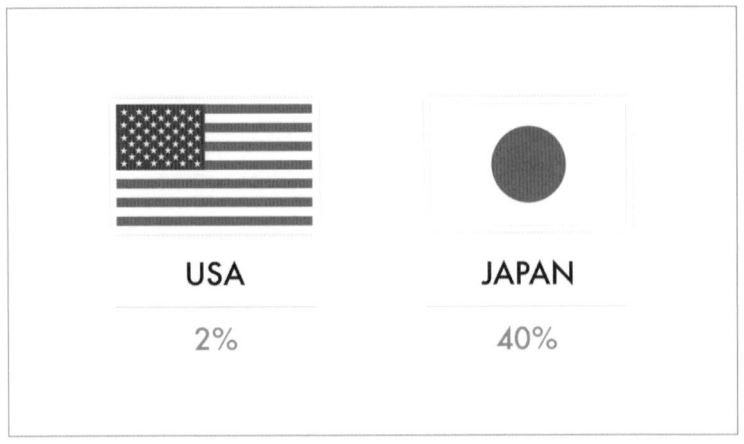

USA	JAPAN
2%	40%

Struggle is a biological requirement for greatness.

Travis asked, "How good are the coaches at making you struggle?" The team shook their heads and said, "Really f'ing good."

That repositioned coaching and struggle. If someone wasn't getting something right away, we were trying to change their response.

Instead of saying, "I'm doing bad," replace that with, "I'm getting better."

That's a different energy in which everyone operates.

The takeaway from this PGM: We have to grow toward our goals (which requires struggle).

PGM: GROWTH > OUTCOME

In 2017, Gonzaga went to the Final Four. During a team film session, guess who walked in?

Kobe Bryant. How cool is that?

The team did a 15-minute Q and A with him.

Some of the guys who had been on that roster were still on the team and obviously connected to that experience.

One of the things that makes Kobe *Kobe*, is his insatiable curiosity. We wanted to explore that together.

To kick off this PGM, this book was on each player's chair:

Travis didn't really talk about the book. It was just something for them to explore on their own. Travis would have sidebar conversations with the guys based on what stood out to them. But there was no homework.

After they took their seats, Travis put this up on the screen:

DO YOU:

LOVE TO WIN OR **HATE TO LOSE**

He asked, "Do you love to win or hate to lose?" The majority said, "Hate to lose."

Then Travis asked them, "What do you think Kobe Bryant is?"

"Hate to lose," they said.

Travis then showed the team a clip from a BET interview that Jemele Hill did with Kobe Bryant.

> **Jemele:** *"There's two types of players, players who love to win and players who hate to lose. Which one are you?"*

> **Kobe:** *"I'm neither. Meaning that I play to figure things out. I play to learn something. Because if you play with a fear of failure or you play with the will to win, it's a weakness either way."*

> **Jemele:** *"A lot of people in general are afraid of failure. How did you become one of the people who doesn't seem to be afraid of failing?"*

Kobe: *"It doesn't exist, it's nonexistent. What the hell does that mean? I mean seriously, what does failure mean? It doesn't exist. It's a figment of your imagination."*

To see more of this inteview, watch Brett's talk at kobe.whatdriveswinning.com

Kobe has created an alternate reality.

Failure doesn't exist there. Why? To Kobe, the only way you can fail is to not progress. That's a next-level mentality.

Travis asked the team, "What if you prioritized growth over outcome?"

For some, winning isn't enough. They need to feel like they're progressing toward mastery of their craft. The Gonzaga team compared Kobe Bryant to Brad Stevens.

They acknowledged that both had the next-level mentality, but it manifested itself in such different ways.

The team reviewed Brad's quote after his third-year contract extension:

"We'll continue striving for growth in pursuit of Banner 18."

Banner 18 is the goal.

Striving for growth is the purpose.

They thought back to the blank banner that hangs from the rafters inside their arena and practice facility; a visual representation of their goal.

BOSTON CELTICS 1957 WORLD CHAMPIONS	BOSTON CELTICS 1959 WORLD CHAMPIONS	BOSTON CELTICS 1960 WORLD CHAMPIONS	BOSTON CELTICS 1961 WORLD CHAMPIONS	BOSTON CELTICS 1962 WORLD CHAMPIONS	BOSTON CELTICS 1963 WORLD CHAMPIONS
BOSTON CELTICS 1964 WORLD CHAMPIONS	BOSTON CELTICS 1965 WORLD CHAMPIONS	BOSTON CELTICS 1966 WORLD CHAMPIONS	BOSTON CELTICS 1968 WORLD CHAMPIONS	BOSTON CELTICS 1969 WORLD CHAMPIONS	BOSTON CELTICS 1974 WORLD CHAMPIONS
BOSTON CELTICS 1976 WORLD CHAMPIONS	BOSTON CELTICS 1981 WORLD CHAMPIONS	BOSTON CELTICS 1984 WORLD CHAMPIONS	BOSTON CELTICS 1986 WORLD CHAMPIONS	BOSTON CELTICS 2008 WORLD CHAMPIONS	#18

But if you go inside the Celtics' weight room, you'll see this:

Kaizen is painted on their beams. Kaizen means *small incremental change*. It's a visual cue that represents *striving for growth*. And to grow, according to Brad Stevens, you must have accountability. When Brad took over at Butler, there were five core values. He added a sixth.

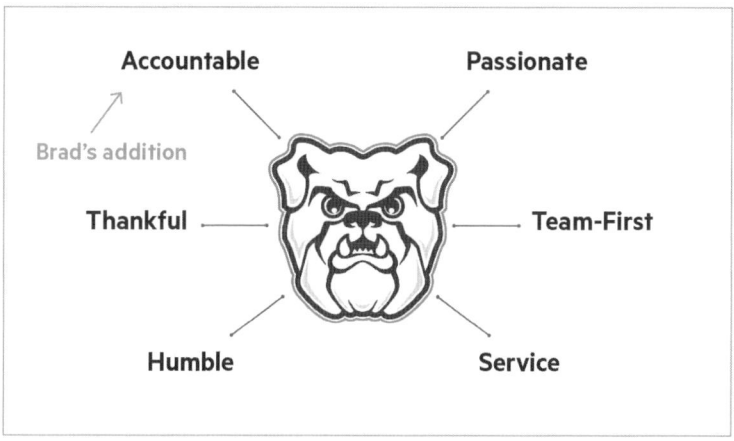

In his mind, the only way you could grow was to be *accountable*.

That was a topic that Mark Few wanted us to discuss with the team next.

PGM: YOU NEED ALL THREE

Gonzaga had the #1 offense in the country. But they were ranked 68th defensively.

In practices and post-games, the coaches focused on the defensive ranking as opposed to the offensive ranking, because it wasn't up to par for the goals they set.

It would be easy for the guys to feel like their offensive performance was being taken for granted and that they were constantly being picked on for their defense.

The conversation that Travis and I had on how to approach this PGM about accountability centered around these questions:

How do you have a conversation about accountability without it feeling like propaganda from the coaching staff?

How do you introduce accountability into the environment while protecting the positive, family feel that they were cultivating?

Here's how we approached the conversation.

The guys love competition, so Travis divided the team into three groups of four to five people.

Then, he assigned each group to one of these three categories:

Each group had to come up with a pros/cons list for their category. After five minutes, they would then present their list to the team. When they finished presenting, the team would try to add to their pros/cons list.

Whichever group had the least number of add-ons won the competition. Because there was an element of competition, the alpha personalities began debating over accountability.

It was beautiful...and important.

If you do this with your team, these are some of the answers that you will see:

COACH-POLICED TEAMS

PROS	CONS
Clear line of authority	One set of eyes
Understands vision	Limited time with team
Takes pressure off of players having to confront peers	Players can get numb to your voice

TEAM-POLICED TEAMS

PROS	CONS
More sets of eyes watching	Can disrupt friendships
Collective increase in ownership	Requires closeness
Peer pressure has powerful influence	Focuses on things outside your control: Teammates' behavior

PROS	CONS
Prepares you for life	Blindspots harder to reveal
You're with yourself 24/7	Easier to take shortcuts
You're in control of your own actions	Judge self on intent & judge others on actions

Once the team finished, Travis asked, "What's the biggest takeaway?"

They had two:

1.) "We need all three."

2.) "The quality of the relationships determines the quality of the accountability."

It was an incredible conversation, and it started to make sense why we were doing PGMs. The conversations were building a brotherhood based on substance.

The accountability PGM took the team up to the most prestigious tournament of the pre-season: The Maui Invitational.

Up until then, the country's conversation around college basketball was centered around two questions:

1.) Who would win a game between the Duke Blue Devils (college) and the Cleveland Cavaliers (pro)?

2.) How good is Zion Williamson (Duke player)?

Duke and Gonzaga met in the championship of this tournament and Gonzaga won.

The conversation shifted to:

1.) How good is Gonzaga?

2.) How good is Rui?

Gonzaga replaced Duke as #1 in the AP poll, and things became more chaotic.

Gonzaga had two big non-conference matchups in December and the coaches wanted to shore up basketball deficiencies.

So guess what took a back seat?

Personal Growth Mondays.

The team had a joke: Instead of the conversations being called PGMs, they became PGTBD (to be decided).

In the coming weeks, Gonzaga lost to a great Tennessee team on a neutral court. They then went to the University of North Carolina and lost there. The team had taken a few steps backward right before it was time for my second visit.

SECOND VISIT

F.A.M.I.L.Y.

F.A.M.I.L.Y.

When I came to campus the second time, I met with the four influencers of the locker room. They shared with me that PGMs started out as a priority but got lost in the shuffle.

The goal became to build back some momentum around those conversations. It was perfect timing because it was mid-December when we connected, and the players were out of class.

We had more time to explore why the outside noise created distractions and how the adversity started to tear at the brotherhood beneath the surface.

This PGM took a little longer than the usual 15 minutes. It lasted 30 minutes. We needed to have a high impact to try and get things back on track inside that room.

The first thing I did was give them a sheet of paper and I asked them to draw a line down the middle of it.

On the left side, I asked them to write down the answer to this question: How does society determine your success as a player? (Each player listed out five answers.)

Here are the top five answers that showed up:

- Stats
- Winning
- Social Media (followers, likes)
- Awards
- Highlights

As soon as they finished that exercise, we went to the right side of the paper. I asked them one question, ten times.

Each time, they wrote down what answer came to mind—the question was about life in general.

I asked, "What's important to you?"

Here's an example of an individual's top ten answers:

- Family
- Friends
- God
- Success
- Winning
- Happiness
- Health
- Peace of Mind
- Relationships
- Growth

Once they finished writing their ten, I had them prioritize their top five. And then we compared what's really important to them against society's scorecard.

Society's Scorecard:	What's Really Important:
Stats	Family
Winning	Friends
Social Media	God
Awards	Happiness
Highlights	Peace of Mind

I asked them, "What's your biggest takeaway?"

It was clear to them that their values were very different from society's.

The key: If we listen to society, it's going to pull us away from what's really important.

They could feel that starting to happen.

I wanted to share a story with Gonzaga about a team that I worked with in the past (the 2016 University of Florida softball team) that experienced some of the things that they were going through. It was amazing to see how Gonzaga connected to this.

When I began my work with the Florida softball team, they were coming off of back-to-back National Championships.

The five returning seniors wanted to three-peat. They told me that they wanted their mantra to be "brick by brick."

As soon as they said that, I immediately thought of a reference from a TED talk by Margaret Heffernan called *Forget The Pecking Order At Work.*

Margaret Heffernan
"Forget the Pecking Order at Work"

When the going gets tough, and it always will get tough if you're doing breakthrough work that really matters, what people need is social support. And they need to know who to ask for help....

What motivates people are the bonds and loyalty and trust they develop between each other.

What matters is the mortar, not just the bricks.

Mortar is what makes bricks bond together.

Around the time of the team watching that video, ESPN interviewed Kirsti Merritt (Florida outfielder) and asked her, "What does Florida need to do to three-peat?"

Here's how she answered.

Kirsti Merritt
Florida

For Florida to win another national championship, we have to unite.

When Kirsti said that, we combined her quote with the idea from the TED Talk. The team saw this banner every time they came to and from the facility:

Everything we did from that point forward was going to be about building mortar.

To illustrate the importance of mortar, Tim Walton (Florida's head softball coach) handed out a brick to everybody on the team. He then had them do an activity.

On one side of the brick, they wrote their name with a sharpie. On the other, they wrote one word that represented what they were going to bring to the team.

Each person had to explain why they chose the word that they did. It became very emotional because the team took it seriously.

Once everyone finished sharing, Tim asked the team to build a wall using their bricks.

When the wall was built, Tim called on a senior to come up and push the wall over. Here's what the bricks looked like after the wall was pushed over:

His teaching point was: When we get knocked down, do we separate?

After he asked the team to think about that, he instructed them to go and grab their bricks. Tim then asked them to build the wall a second time. This time, using mortar. (This was also symbolic to Gonzaga because they were rebuilding toward #1 after being knocked down.)

Earlier that day, Tim called a few of the "Brickies" in Gainesville, Florida, to learn how to mix concrete and make mortar.

The team rebuilt the wall a second time with some intentionality. They put all of the seniors' bricks on top because they were the most invested in the program, and they had the most to lose.

After they finished, this is what it looked like:

The takeaway from the activity: If we get knocked down, *we're not separating*. It stood in the middle of the locker room as a visual cue: *It's All About The Mortar*.

Tim could feel the expectations weighing down the team, so here's what he did next. He contacted all of the parents and asked them to send in two childhood pictures of their daughters.

One picture in the uniform. The other picture had to be outside the uniform.

Then, he created a video where he showed the team pictures of themselves when they were little.

The five seniors:

Aubree Munro

Kelsey Stewart

Kirsti Merritt

Taylor Schwarz

Taylore Fuller

After those pictures cycled through, the video then showed clips of the athletes playing at the University of Florida before ending with this quote:

Somewhere behind the athlete you've become and the hours of practices and the coaches who have pushed you...is a little girl who fell in love with the game...and never looked back... play for her. — Mia Hamm

It was incredibly moving.

Tim is relatively unemotional, but he was moved to tears (as was everyone in the room).

Tim's message: "Think back to when you were a kid. All you cared about was the flavor of popsicle that you were going to get. You didn't care what your batting average was or if you got on base. It was all about having fun with your friends."

The expectations made this about something much different than it was. Those expectations were robbing them of the joy that they once felt.

The entire team connected to that feeling (as did Gonzaga).

Tim was trying to remind them where that joy comes from and how to get them to play with that kind of energy.

He created a poster board that had a brick wall on it, and in the center it said *Moments*. It looked like this:

He then handed out *Moment Cards* that looked like this:

Everybody wrote down their favorite moment of the season up until that point (they were just entering postseason).

After they finished writing, each person (including coaches) got up in front of the team and shared why they picked the moment they did. Once they finished, they taped it up onto the poster board. The result:

That board illustrated all the moments that cemented this group together. It reinforced why they were ready for postseason.

Let's fast-forward to the final play of the season.

The situation:

All Florida had to do was get one out and they'd extend the series and regain momentum. Unfortunately for them, this happened:

Georgia hit a walk-off home run.

The seniors' worst fear was losing their last game in their jersey.

That happened.

Moments after Georgia hit the walk-off, Florida's catcher Aubree Munro was interviewed.

Aubree Munro
Florida

Yeah that ball was hit pretty well. But with Kirsti in center field, you know there's always a chance. I mean from since the day we got here...(choking up)

Since the day we got here, Kirsti has been the player that would go through the wall.

So her literally going through the wall to try and rob that to give our team a chance, really kind of just shows you what Kirsti is about.

It shows you what our team is about.

It shows that even though that ball was hit really well, we still thought that we had a chance with Kirsti in center.

She's one of my best friends and I'm happy to have played with her for four years.

After the players finished with the media, they went back into the locker room. Tim, as the head coach, stuck around for more interviews. When he finished, he went to a separate coach's locker room to shower off and change.

After he got dressed, he got a knock on the door from his wife, Sam.

She said that the team was still in the locker room.

Nobody wanted to leave that room because they knew when they exited, that was the end of that team.

Tim went back into the team locker room where everybody was waiting to share their final thoughts and one last moment.

Every time they break the huddle, they say FAMILY.

Here's what that means to them: **F**orget **A**bout **M**e **I** **L**ove **Y**ou.

The 2016 Florida softball team got knocked down...but they didn't separate. Which shows that they achieved this:

When I shared that with the Gonzaga men's basketball team, it felt as if they were looking at themselves in the mirror.

They knew that when they were at their best, their mortar was strong. They made a commitment to each other after seeing this talk that they were not going to let anything tear at the brotherhood. They were going to withstand whatever came their way.

The momentum for PGMs was back, and we didn't miss another one the entire year.

PGM: THE RETURN

What can divide talented teams? Playing time.

When Gonzaga beat Duke to win the Maui tournament, two of their contributors did not play.

Killian Tillie, a 6'10'' shooter, was projected as a first-round NBA draft pick before his injury; Geno Crandall, a grad transfer, fractured his right hand and missed nine games.

We knew that they were going to be coming back in January, and we wanted to be proactive for this moment:

When Geno and Killian checked in, the fans gave them a standing ovation.

Imagine being the players who are subbed out and seeing the reaction of the arena. That's the stuff that could tear at the mortar.

Here's how we attacked it before it happened.

Do you remember the 2018 National Championship football game? It featured Alabama and Georgia.

ESPN produced a video that showed Alabama's chances to win throughout the game.

57%: At the beginning of the game
17%: When Georgia scored to go up 13-0
7%: When Tagovailoa threw an interception
44%: When Alabama scored their first touchdown
87%: When Alabama lined up for a game-winning field goal from 36 yards out
53%: At the start of overtime
76%: When Alabama had a 2nd and 26 from the 41-yard line
100%: When Alabama scored the final touchdown

After showing that clip to the team, Travis asked, "What makes teams stick together when they only have a 7% chance to win?"

As they were thinking, Travis then showed them this picture from that game.

He asked, "What do you see when you guys look at this?"

The team pointed out that Jalen Hurts (on the left):

1.) Was 25-2 at the time as a starting QB
2.) Led them to a National Championship game the
   year before
3.) Was the SEC Offensive Player of the Year
   (2016-17 season)
4.) Only threw one interception that whole year
   (2017-18 season)

The team also pointed out that at halftime, being down 13-0, the Alabama coaching staff decided to sub in a freshman who had played limited minutes (Tua Tagovailoa) over the sophomore leader in Jalen Hurts.

That picture was Jalen's response. It was a powerful image for the team.

Travis ended the PGM with this question:

What makes a teammate want to run through a wall for you?

Here were Gonzaga's answers:

1.) Respect for them
2.) Trust he would do the same for me
3.) Love. F.A.M.I.L.Y.
4.) Deep relationship
5.) Same unifying purpose

(Number three shows you how much the Florida softball message resonated.)

Travis is always looking for ways to reinforce the message.

The next day when the guys walked into the weight room, this is what they saw:

Each person has to go to that TV to read their workout for the day.

Think about the visual imagery. There's something behind the plan (their workout for the day) that's driving it—the brotherhood.

PGM: A HIGHER STANDARD

When you have a lot of talent on your team, playing time isn't the only issue that's created. Despite their non-Power 5 conference getting better, Gonzaga could win with B- or C-level execution because of their talent.

There's two challenges with that:

1.) It's possible for outcomes to reinforce bad habits.

2.) Motivation can be a challenge when you know you're going to crush a team.

To combat those challenges, Travis showed the team a clip from an interview I did with Bill Beswick, a world-renowned performance psychologist based in the United Kingdom.

Bill Beswick
Sports Psychologist

There was a situation set up in a medical school where people training to be surgeons had to take their final examination—a three-hour examination.

But the professor came into the room and to the surprise of all the students, offered them the opportunity for a B grade without taking the examination.

And all the class, apart from two, stood up and left (and went for a beer hopefully).

They celebrated because all they needed was a B grade to pass their final. So they were clear, they were surgeons, they were professionals.

But two people stayed.

And the professor said, "I've offered you a B grade without taking the examination. Why are you still sitting there?"

And the answer for one of them, I could never forget it.

"I base my life on trying to be an A grade student, an A grade surgeon, an A grade person. I'm not in the mood to accept B grade now. I'll take the examination."

What was the real test?

Who is going to hold themselves to a higher standard than what is required? That's what is going to make you a world-class surgeon.

The discussion with the team evolved into this. Are we going to hold ourselves to a higher standard than the outcome requires?

Because C-level effort will win us games.

Guess what happened the next game?

Their average margin of victory in conference was 27 points.

That checked this box:

    ☑   Regular Season WCC Championship

They chased down this goal:

    ☑   Top 10 Offensive/Defensive Efficiency

This took some effort because right after Maui, they were ranked 120th defensively. By the end of the year, they were ranked fifth. They stayed #1 in offense the entire year.

That A-level consistency earned them #1 in the AP poll, for the second time, right before their conference tournament started.

THIRD VISIT
WATER THE BAMBOO

WATER THE BAMBOO

The week before I arrived for my third visit, Gonzaga lost to St. Mary's in the conference tournament championship.

They had their worst offensive performance of the year and lost 60-47. (Earlier in the year, they beat St. Mary's 94-46.)

Their performance was totally out of character, so how do you handle that with the PGM? How do you not let one outlying performance create doubt?

When we got together, I flashed this graphic up on the screen:

The Golden State Warriors played the Los Angeles Lakers. During that game, Stephen Curry had his worst shooting performance from the three-point line up until that point in his career.

He went 0-10.

We watched a clip of him missing all ten shots back to back to back.

As soon as the video ended, I flashed this graphic up on the screen:

The next game, three days later, the Golden State Warriors played the New Orleans Pelicans. Steph Curry went 13-17 from the three-point line.

We watched all 13 makes. That shooting performance set an NBA record for most three pointers made.

I then showed this graphic:

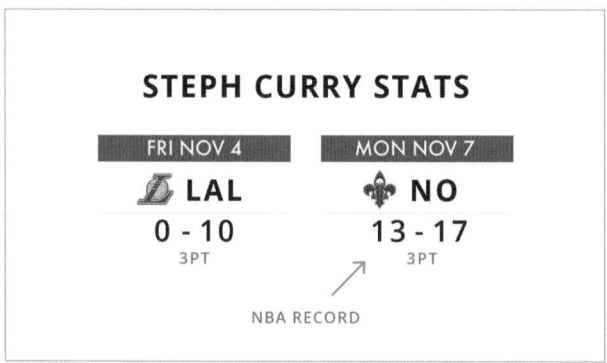

What's the takeaway?

Take a look at this moment from the game on Friday:

This is Steph's tenth shot. At this point in time, he's 0-9. How much time is on the shot clock? 18 seconds. Look at the challenge from the defender on the shot.

Steph is still hunting his shot like normal.

What does that mean?

There's a deep sense of belief in himself. Steph is unwavering despite missing nine shots in a row. That confidence is a large part of why he bounced back the way he did.

That's how we addressed the out-of-character performance by Gonzaga.

It was a quick PGM (4 minutes).

As soon as we wrapped with Steph, I wanted to take a look back at all of the things that the team covered.

I flashed them all on the screen:

We quickly touched on each to recall the conversations, then asked each player to rank his top three PGMs in order of which resonated with him most.

Here's what's interesting: every PGM was represented in their answers. What does that show? Messages resonate differently for each person. It also speaks to the consistency of Travis' facilitation.

The team's overall takeaway of the PGMs was this:

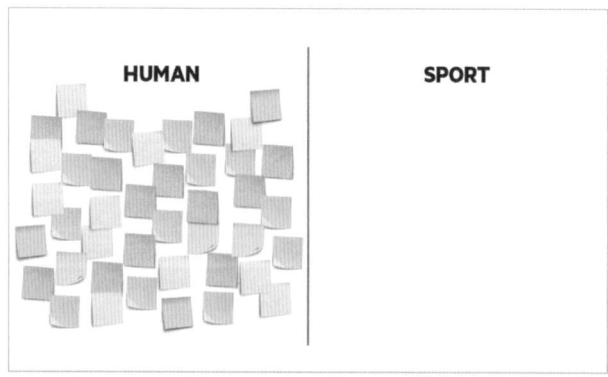

The team didn't avoid what would get in their way, they confronted it head on.

They went on to win the first three rounds of the NCAA tournament before losing in the Elite Eight, to the eventual national runner-up Texas Tech, in an epic, heavyweight battle.

It's really easy to look at an unchecked box and feel like you have failed.

☐   National Championship

That's why having a head coach like Mark Few, who has incredible perspective, is a gift.

When I met with Mark prior to the season starting, we were working on a project, and I asked him a question that I ask a lot of coaches: "Would a championship validate you?"

It's always interesting to me to see how coaches navigate this question. Most will give you lofty, philosophical answers. Very few will answer the way Mark Few did.

Mark Few
Gonzaga

No. I need my kids to eventually say they love their mom and dad and respect everybody out there in the world.

And have our players look back and say they enjoyed the heck out of playing at Gonzaga. I'm pretty much good with that.

He barely answered the question. Where'd he take it?

What's important to him—his family and his players. Mark doesn't give disproportionate value to achievement; he's able to keep sight of what matters—no matter the stage.

He answered that question with just the two of us in a room together. But he's the same guy regardless of the platform.

Here's proof.

In 2017, when Gonzaga won in the Sweet Sixteen and they were 40 minutes away from playing in the program's first Final Four, a reporter asked Mark this question.

"You're 40 minutes away from the Final Four. What would it mean for you to finally get that monkey off your back?" (Compare his answer to what he said to me.)

Mark Few
Gonzaga

First of all, I don't know that I have a monkey on my back.

I don't certainly wake up with one. Or walk around with one.

I don't think these guys (motioning to his players sitting next to him) think I have one.

I don't think my wife thinks I have one.

Or anybody in my family.

And close friends. Fishing buddies never talk about it.

Those are the only people that really matter to me.

Events don't validate the seasoned Mark Few.

Think back to what he said to me. He wanted his players to think about their Gonzaga experience and positively reflect on that.

Josh Perkins was a five-year guy for Gonzaga. He led the team at the point guard position.

Josh and Mark would occasionally butt heads because Josh is somewhat of an artist, and Mark is more of an engineer, which leads to an inherent conflict at times.

Minutes after Gonzaga lost in the Elite Eight to Texas Tech, Josh was asked, "What are you going to miss most?" With tears in his eyes, he answered.

Josh Perkins
Gonzaga

Being around these guys, honestly (pointing to coaches and teammates). There's countless memories I can't even put in words.

Just being with them on a daily basis: road trips, being coached by such high-character guys, playing with their family, their kids. It's a family atmosphere.

You know, I'm going into the real world now (choking up). Best five years of my life. So I'm feeling it right now for sure.

That's what matters to Mark Few.

When Josh says, "I'm going into the real world," that's what Gonzaga's philosophy is built on. They have a saying that's really important to them.

Water the Bamboo.

When you plant the bamboo seed, the seed doesn't sprout for four years.

You water it and you water it and you water it and you don't see the results.

There's no immediate return above ground.

Meanwhile, a root system is taking form underneath the surface.

So when it does sprout, the tree has a root system that will support its growth.

The bamboo tree is the quickest to grow to 90 feet (roughly two feet per day).

That's why Gonzaga's philosophy is *Water the Bamboo.*

As players move on to the next phase of their lives, the goal is for them to have a root system that will support their growth.

And if you go into the weight room, you'll see this...

...a wall made from bamboo.

THE PGM ROAD MAP

1. COMMIT
Consistency communicates commitment. For Gonzaga, when Personal Growth Mondays became Personal Growth *To Be Decided*, the players felt that. Protect the space.

2. PLAN
What's the team need? Every Sunday night, Travis and I tried to answer that question to determine what media assets were going to be used and what questions Travis was going to ask.

3. FACILITATE
As the facilitator, it's not about having the answers. It's about asking the right questions. Travis realized the less he talked, the better the PGM, because it gave space for the team to find its voice.

4. REINFORCE
The message doesn't take root unless you revisit it. Whether it's visual cues, text messages, or personal conversations, Travis is finding ways to *Water the Bamboo* and springboard into the next conversation.

To learn more about how Travis Knight implemented PGMs, visit Zags.WhatDrivesWinning.com.

PART 3

OREGON WOMEN'S BASKETBALL

PhD IN ELEVATING YOUR TEAMMATES

Sabrina Ionescu, the leader of the Oregon women's basketball team, had the ball in this situation:

Sabrina drove left. Stepped back. Hit a three, and the crowd went nuts.

That shot helped lead Oregon to the program's first ever Final Four.

A few hours later, Sabrina tweeted:

My first meeting with Sabrina started with this question: "What's your biggest personal struggle that not many people know about?"

Sabrina explained how she had a difficult time trusting other people and how it was hard for her to build strong relationships. That challenge leaked over into the relationships that she had with her teammates.

Sabrina would ask herself, "Who's going to be able to go to war with me when it matters most?"

When she shared that with me, I thought back to an interview that I did with Maya Moore.

Maya is regarded as one of the best basketball players of all time, and she played for the greatest coach in her sport: Geno Auriemma at the University of Connecticut.

I asked Maya, "What's the best lesson you learned from Geno?"

I showed her response to Sabrina.

Maya Moore
WNBA

If you want to lead others, you have to have a relationship with them.

You have to be willing to put yourself out there to get to know people if you want to lead them.

Be real, be honest, and be yourself.

And don't be afraid to show some weakness sometimes in order to create better chemistry and build a bond.

Because they're going to do everything they can for you, if you show them that you want to be there for them.

Sabrina has not been trained to show weakness. She's not been trained to be vulnerable. Sabrina is a competitive machine.

Because her teammates are human beings and not just human doings, when Sabrina pulls the curtain back and exposes her real self to her teammates (not just her performer self), a deeper connection can form.

Next, I showed Sabrina a clip from Geno Auriemma on a lesson he tries to get all his leaders to understand.

Geno Auriemma
Connecticut

If you're going to lead, you better have somebody that is dying to follow you.

A lot of great players think that, "If I just come out here and I work hard and bust my butt, of course they'll follow me."

They may or they may not.

But if you make them feel like you will do anything for them, then they will follow you.

If they think you're doing all this just for you, at some point they're going to go, "Nah."

So, you got to get them first to respect you, and love you, and feel in their heart for you.

Then they will fall on their sword for you.

I asked Sabrina, "Are you the hardest worker on the team?"

She said, "Yeah."

"Will anybody ever match you?"

"No."

So what does that mean?

Nobody on the team is going to match Sabrina with their work output. Why? If they do, she will just do more—which shows that a gap will always exist.

How the leader handles that gap is essential. If you're the best player, it can feel like you are carrying the team.

If the leader gets angry about that or resents it, the team is losing. People feel that energy. The goal is to lift, not suppress.

I asked Sabrina what she took away from Geno.

1.) Just because you work hard doesn't mean people will follow.

2.) Relationships matter.

Sabrina had the power due to her visibility. Because of that, she needed to pursue the relationships with her teammates.

We looked at how Geno does that with his team.

Geno Auriemma
Connecticut

I try to make everything that we do personal.

It's never about UCONN.

Who cares about this stuff?

One of the best questions I asked my players is, "If I took this logo off your chest, would you play any different?"

And they look at me, I go, "Hell no."

"I could put any logo on here and you would not play any different. Why? You ain't playing for this. You're not playing for UCONN. You're not playing for our dorms, our apartments, our library. You're not playing for any of that.

You know who you play for?

Your teammates.

Because they are the most important people in your life, and you want them to go back to their apartment, close their eyes, and go, 'Man, I don't know where I would be without so and so. I don't know how we could ever win without her. I don't want to be on anybody else's team but hers.'

That's what you want your teammates to say.

Not like, 'I really like her. She's a great kid. She's fun to be around.'

Well what do you think about her as a teammate?

'You can't win with her, coach.'

What do you want them to say when they close their eyes?"

I asked Sabrina, "What do you think?"

"I love Geno," Sabrina said. "He's right though. Put any logo on my chest and I wouldn't play any different. I bring what I bring."

I asked her, "What do you want your teammates to think about you when they close their eyes at night?"

"That I elevate them," Sabrina said.

And that became the centerpiece of our discussions. The next night, they played Mississippi State at home and ESPN ran a feature on our meeting. Holly Rowe said, "Sabrina is going to get her PhD in Elevating Her Teammates."

Sabrina sent it to me. We generated some momentum. We agreed that anytime I came to campus I would connect with her first to talk about different ways to elevate her teammates.

Then, after Sabrina and I finished our meeting, I would facilitate a conversation with the team.

Here's an example of a team conversation that happened later in the year.

THE NAPKINS

This meeting took place in February after Oregon lost their second game in a row.

Here's how it ended: 12 seconds left, Oregon was down by three and UCLA was shooting a free throw. Sabrina looked to one of her teammates and said, "Box out."

UCLA missed the free throw, the ball got back-tapped out, UCLA recovered, and Sabrina had to foul them to stop the clock.

It was her fifth foul.

Before exiting the court, Sabrina walked over to her teammate, pushed her and said, "You had one job."

Then she walked off the court and someone handed her a Gatorade bottle.

She threw it down and it exploded.

She walked past the bench into the tunnel, while the game was still going on.

I arrived on campus a few days later. Sabrina and I had a two-and-a-half-hour conversation.

Initially Sabrina was thinking, "They're lucky I didn't do more."

Eventually, Sabrina got to a place where she could see how her teammates could think that she walked out on them. She said, "I'd like to address the team."

The next day, when we met with the team, Sabrina kicked off the meeting: "I could see how you guys could think I walked out on you." She then asked the team, "What do you guys need from me? How could I be a better leader for each of you?"

And then one of the coolest moments I've ever been a part of happened.

Satou Sabally raised her hand.

Satou is an amazing player and an incredible influence in the locker room.

She's 6' 4" from Berlin, Germany. Satou can be strong and comforting in the same moment.

She said, "Sabrina, I'm disappointed in you that you pushed our teammate."

Then she looked at her teammate and said, "I'm disappointed in you that you didn't confront Sabrina."

Then she said, "I'm disappointed in me that I didn't confront Sabrina."

Lastly, she confronted the rest of the team and said, "And I'm disappointed in all of you because nobody did...*we were all in our own tunnel*."

She ended by addressing the team. "Sabrina is asking us what she can do, which will add more pressure. Our job is to take pressure off of her."

Think about this: When Sabrina asked the team, "What do you need from me?" that was opening a scary door for her—one that put her in a vulnerable place.

She threw a Gatorade bottle and walked out of the arena while the game was going on. Think about how some teams would handle that situation. How did Oregon handle it?

They treated her with incredible love, care, and acceptance.

Instead of using the platform to blame, they used that platform to reflect on how they could have helped her deal with it. They looked to the inside and what they could control.

As Satou finished, Erin Boley (a quiet, consistent, shooting assassin) raised her hand and said, "I think we should all come up with one thing that we could each commit to the team for the rest of the season."

When Erin added to what Satou said, that unloaded pressure for Sabrina. That's Erin saying, *We got you, Sab.*

That's how critical the first followers can be for bridge-building.

Here's what they did next. Satou said, "I always thought if you really love someone, you should be able to tell them your fears."

Satou asked the team to get up from their seats and move to the back of the locker room so they could sit in a circle.

She then asked the team two questions:

What is your biggest fear in basketball? And in life?

Everybody answered the question about basketball first. You could feel the authenticity in the room.

Some of the answers:

"Managing expectations"
"I feel like I don't add value"
"My parents are so wrapped up in this"

After everybody answered, they moved to the next question. It was deep stuff that brought tears to everyone in the room.

At one point, Satou had to go get a box of napkins so people could wipe their tears.

The overwhelming feeling was, "I'm with you every day and I had no idea that you were going through that."

When everybody finished answering, I thanked them for allowing me to be a part of the conversation. I felt like it was most appropriate if they closed the meeting without me.

I left, and 25 minutes later they grabbed me in the hallway to tell me what they'd done.

They combined Satou and Erin's ideas—everybody on the team

committed to one thing that they were going to bring to the team for the rest of the season.

On the napkins that contained their tears, the team wrote their words.

They hung the napkins on a whiteboard inside their locker room to create a visual reminder.

They shared with me that they wanted their postseason theme to be *Rise Above*.

The goal would be to create a postseason package that would be divided into sections to mirror the bracket of March Madness.

Weekend One: Round of 64 / 32
Weekend Two: Round of 16 / 8
Weekend Three: The Final Four

Let's get into the messaging for weekend one.

FIRST WEEKEND
ASSURANCE / 95%

ASSURANCE

The next time Sabrina and I met would be in preparation for March Madness.

The team had just lost to Stanford in the PAC 12 Tournament Championship game, 64-57. At that point in time, Sabrina started to feel doubt creep in.

She texted me prior to our meeting, expressing some of the doubts she had about the team.

The word Sabrina chose to commit to bring to the team was *assurance* (give confidence). She wanted to be self-assured and deal assurance to the team.

When I met with her individually, I brought a clip about Diana Taurasi to build on the theme of how to *Elevate Her Teammates*.

Sabrina likes the way Geno Auriemma's mind works, and he talked about what made Diana the best player of all time.

After each point he made about Diana, I would pause the video and ask Sabrina a question related to what he had just said.

Geno's 1st Point: *"There was never a time Diana stepped out on the floor where she didn't think that she was the best player on the floor, regardless of what the occasion was."*

I asked Sabrina, "Do you feel like you are the best player regardless of the competition?"

Sabrina said, "No." Sabrina's Score: 0 for 1.

Geno's 2nd Point: *"Diana never doubted that she would win."*

I asked Sabrina, "Do you know you're going to win?"

Sabrina said, "No." Sabrina's Score: 0-2.

Geno's 3rd Point: *"Diana never doubted that if something bad happened, that she could fix it."*

I asked, "Can you fix any problem?"

Sabrina said, "Yes," to this one. Sabrina's Score: 1-3.

Geno's 4th Point: *"Diana convinced every one of her teammates to be like that."*

I paused the video and asked, "Do you convince your teammates to believe those things?"

Sabrina said, "No." She knew that they could feel her doubt. Sabrina's Score: 1-4.

What Geno said next really resonated with her.

Geno Auriemma
Connecticut

There might have been kids on Diana's team that were wondering, "Am I any good? Can I really do that?"

And Diana would go, "Sure you can. You can do this, this, this, exactly what I'm telling you to do. You're going to be able to do it."

Now, what she didn't tell you is, "The reason you're going to be able to do it is because I'm on the team, so you're not going to have a choice, but if you struggle I'll bail you out."

And that kind of groundswell that she created just put everybody over the top.

As soon as the video ended, Sabrina had a sigh of relief. She felt like Geno was talking directly to her. That recalibrated her—Sabrina was ready for the postseason. It was time to talk to the team.

95%

Sabrina started off the next team meeting saying, "I think we are all feeling a lot of pressure. For some, it might be nice to have some relief. I'm asking you to commit for three more weeks."

After she said that, to build on the *Rise Above* theme, I showed the movie trailer for *Free Solo*.

It's an incredible movie about a mountain climber who climbs without ropes.

In other words, if he falls, he dies.

Most people who take part in free soloing eventually fall to their death. That's part of the conflict for the director. It would be terrible for you to watch your friend fall through the frame to his death.

As soon as the trailer ended, you could tell there were a lot of sweaty palms. They were stunned.

I asked them how that could connect with what they're experiencing together.

"During the regular season, it's kind of like climbing with a rope. If you fall, you get another chance to climb." The team added, "Climbing without a rope is a much different experience because the consequences are higher—much like the postseason, if you fall there's a finality to the team."

And when you are in a win-or-go-home situation, pressure increases.

Pressure creates abnormal behavior.

When we start to feel pressure, things become bigger than they are, like a missed shot.

What was Oregon known for?

The #1 offense in the country. But even the best offensive teams struggle to maintain great shooting for six straight performances over a three-weekend window.

I shared a video clip with the team on how Billy Donovan helped an individual see the big picture when his shot wasn't falling.

He had a player who went 2-11 shooting and played 38 minutes. This player got down on himself when he wasn't playing well—2-11 is not very good.

The next day, Billy walked in and asked the player, "How many shots did you miss last night?"

The player says, "Nine."

"How long does it take for you to shoot a shot?"

The player was a little confused and said, "About a second."

"How many minutes did you play?"

Player says, "38."

"So let me get this straight: You allowed nine seconds to affect the rest of the 37:51 that you played?"

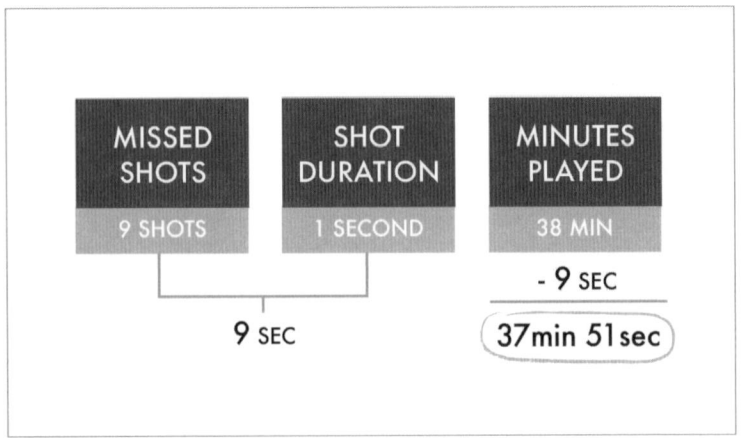

As the clip ended, I asked, "How many of you let the minority affect the majority?"

Everyone's hands went up.

After we addressed that on an individual level, we looked at it from a team perspective.

Billy Donovan
Oklahoma City Thunder

About 95% of the game of basketball is being played without the ball in your hands.

So many of these guys are unable to play their 95% because they are so consumed with their 5%. And their 5% takes them to these incredible emotional highs and lows, based on whether the ball goes in the basket.

You ever see this? When a guy makes a shot, and they're running down the floor saying, "Come on!"

Like, how about when you miss a shot say, "Come on!"

I try to expose the game of basketball for what it is, and try to get them to see what the big picture is in the game.

Making shots is going to come and go. But the things that you can actually have control over are the things you're having to do 95% of the time.

Why not focus on being great at those things?

I asked the team if they'd ever thought about basketball in that way...none of them had (and they've played the sport for a long time).

I then asked, "What's the biggest takeaway?"

In simple terms, they said:

"When we play good, we're big. When we struggle, we shrink."

That explains momentum.

"We need to be big when we're struggling."

They commited to the 95%—all of the things that don't involve the ball.

They knew if they won that battle, they would be able to go toe-to-toe with anyone. They did.

That commitment got them through the first weekend.

WEEKEND ONE

3/24

	Indiana	68
	Oregon	91

3/22

	Oregon	78
	Portland State	40

On to the second weekend...

SECOND WEEKEND

WHAT BREAKS YOU

WHAT BREAKS YOU

What increases each round you advance? Pressure.

Pressure creates abnormal behavior.

I wasn't going to be with the team in person, so I sent three assets to Sabrina that she would share with the team.

The first asset I showed her was a clip from the second round of the men's NCAA Tournament.

Here's the situation: Murray State was a 12 seed playing Florida State, who was a 4 seed.

With just over 11 minutes to go in the first half, the score was:

FSU: 22—MSU: 21

Murray State had a Top-5 draft prospect named Ja Morant. (He went on to be the #2 pick in the 2019 draft.)

At this point in the game, Ja was playing really well, hitting four three-pointers. With 11:33 left to go in the first half, Ja got a rebound, dribbled it up, and got fancy.

He wrapped the ball around his back, faking a pass to a teammate. The crowd *oohed* and *ahhed*.

Ja then threw an uncatchable pass to a teammate.

As Ja transitioned back to defense to stop the fast break from his turnover, we paused the video.

The clip showed him yelling at his teammate with both of his hands up.

I asked, "Who's Ja talking to?"

Sabrina responded, "His teammate."

I then asked, "Where's Ja's mind?"

She responded, "Last play."

Ja's pulling his teammate into the last play.

I let the clip play so Sabrina could see Ja's defensive effort. He passively allowed the Florida State player to get a lightly contested layup. As the ball went through the hoop, Ja was still talking to his teammate—he was *still* on the last play.

At that moment, the score was: FSU: 24—MSU: 21

It ended: FSU: 90—MSU: 62

From that point forward, they were playing against two opponents. Florida State and themselves.

That's what pressure does.

Ja is a tremendous talent who got overwhelmed and didn't handle the moment in a way that helped his team.

The goal for Ja: Learn from that and get better.

The goal for the Oregon's women's basketball team: Don't let that happen to us.

The next clip I showed Sabrina was from Nick Saban, head coach of the University of Alabama football team. In the clip, he explained his definition of mental toughness.

Nick Saban
Alabama

I never really defined toughness for you.

The way I'm going to define toughness to you, because I'm talking about mental toughness, and I think everybody can relate to it is, it's all about what does it take to break you?

And the reason I come to this is we had to put hurricane windows in our house in Florida on the beach.

So I asked the guy, "How do you figure out these windows are better than those windows?"

What does it take to break them?

What does it take to break a team? That's how tough the group is.

The Oregon team knew that the next round would be about stabilizing the storm, which is why I pulled a quote from the movie *The Revenant*.

Earlier in the year, I showed the whole team the trailer.

Throughout the movie, the main character, played by Leonardo DiCaprio, faced near-death experience after near-death experience.

This mantra helped him get through:

"When there is a storm,

And you stand in front of a tree,

If you look at its branches you swear it will fall.

But if you watch the trunk, you will see its stability."

It's powerful imagery. I sent a graphic, with that quote on it, to Sabrina so she could share it with the team as a reminder.

When there is a storm

And you stand in front of a tree

If you look at its branches,
you swear it will fall.

But if you watch the trunk,
you will see its stability.

ESPN ran a small segment right before the Sweet Sixteen game against South Dakota State showcasing where Oregon got their stability. Each player taped their wrists and wrote the word that they had committed to the team (the ones they wrote on the napkins that contained their tears) to stabalize the storm.

The commitment to their words helped them advance to their first ever Final Four.

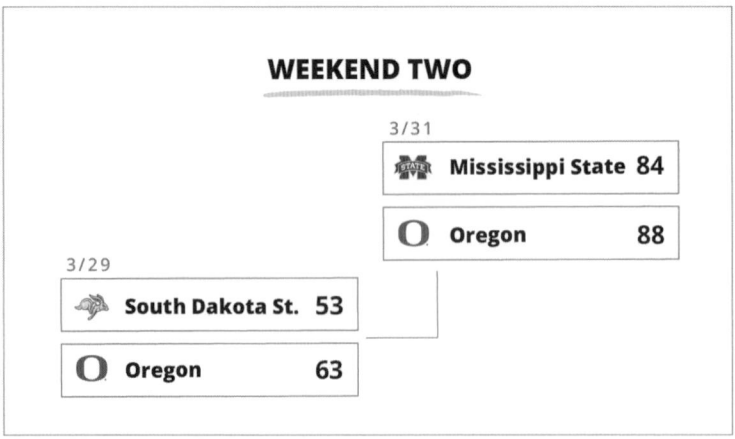

WEEKEND TWO

3/31

Mississippi State **84**

Oregon **88**

3/29

South Dakota St. **53**

Oregon **63**

On to the third weekend...

THIRD WEEKEND

HEAT OR BURN / RISE ABOVE

HEAT OR BURN

Sabrina's all-time favorite player is Kobe Bryant. Kobe has a show called *Detail*. On his show, he broke down Sabrina's game from the Elite Eight. Imagine hearing your favorite player talk about your game. That would be surreal.

Then, Sabrina won the Wade Trophy—National Player of the Year—and they had a big ceremony the night before the Final Four games began.

Sabrina's current favorite player in the NBA is Steph Curry. He was asked what advice he would give to Sabrina and the team.

 "Keep doing it. The team's blazing a new trail for their program. Why not go win it all? She's a legend in her own right," Steph said.

So when Kobe breaks your game down, you win Player of the Year, and your favorite NBA players are paying attention to what you are doing—what can that cause?

Pressure.

Pressure creates abnormal behavior.

Here's how we addressed it.

I showed Sabrina a clip from Game One of the 2018 NBA Finals. The Cleveland Cavaliers were playing the Golden State Warriors. The game was tied at 107 with 4.7 seconds left. The Cavs were at the free-throw line.

George Hill (Cavs player) missed the free-throw that could have put them up one.

J.R. Smith (Cavs player) grabbed the rebound with 4.3 seconds left.

We paused there.

J.R. Smith got an offensive rebound over Kevin Durant, who is nearly seven feet tall. If Kevin got the rebound and called time-out, Golden State could have advanced the ball with 4.3 seconds to get a shot off.

The reason I mention that is that there is something good that comes from the play.

Now, J.R. Smith forgot time and score. He thought they were up one (instead of being tied) so he dribbled the ball the opposite way to run out the clock. Here you can see his teammates' confusion:

There's a replay that shows his teammate, LeBron James, at the top of the key when J.R. got the rebound.

LeBron did three things in those 4.3 seconds:

1.) Called for the ball
2.) Signaled to J.R. he was going the wrong way
3.) Tried to call timeout

There's footage that surfaced that stayed on LeBron and J.R. from that point forward until overtime started.

It was painful to watch.

What does J.R.'s body language tell you right here?

Have you ever let someone down and felt ashamed about it? That's what J.R. is feeling in that picture.

Two minutes go by…and not one word is said by LeBron to J.R. and they're sitting right next to one another.

Let's empathize with LeBron for a second.

Have you been in a situation where you feel like you are carrying a team by yourself and you feel like you are surrounded by people who are not pulling their weight? (Think back to group projects for school.)

At this point in the game, he has 49 points and has played one of his best games ever. All he needed was:

- George Hill (a 10-year veteran) to make a free throw
- J.R. Smith (a 14-year veteran) to know time and score
- Tyronn Lue (coach) to call timeout to regroup

He had single-handedly lifted the Cavs into a position to win against a more talented team, and he was surrounded by mistakes.

It could be easy for LeBron to feel like he was carrying the team.

While waiting for overtime to start, LeBron asked Tyronn, the head coach, "We ain't have no timeouts?"

This is the moment that Tyronn informed him that they did have a timeout and he didn't call it:

A few minutes later, the huddle broke and LeBron walked onto the court. LeBron and J.R. didn't speak the whole time. Nothing productive was discussed.

What happened in that series?

The Cavs were swept 4-0.

The question to ask in that type of situation:

Do you want to be right? Or do you want to be effective?

The only person who could rectify that situation was LeBron. That shows us that the best player has the ability to either heat the building or burn it down.

It's easy for us to look at that and judge LeBron. It's not easy for us to understand the amount of pressure that he had on him. When I showed Sabrina the clip of LeBron, she didn't judge him.

She learned from him.

Sabrina could directly empathize with what he was feeling. She thought back to when she threw the Gatorade bottle and walked into the tunnel.

Her goal: Heat the building, don't burn it down. It was time to address the team.

RISE ABOVE

During the last team meeting, I wanted to show a clip from an interview I did with Jay Wright.

Jay talked about the biggest regret that he had after leading a team to his first Final Four. This is what Jay learned.

Jay Wright
Villanova

In 2009, we reached the Final Four. The celebration afterward at the hotel in Boston was incredible.

As I think about it now, it was comparable back then to winning the national championship in 2016 and 2018.

When we returned to campus and the celebration was done, we were starting to prepare to go to Detroit. I could already sense it in the team, even in myself—there was a sense of accomplishment that was going to take away from our hunger. I wouldn't have admitted it at the time.

I was mad at myself and I even got into it with Scottie Reynolds in practice before we went to the Final Four.

He and I got into an argument because I was trying to get myself and everybody hungry and nasty again.

Brett Ledbetter: *"Was that abnormal, for that particular year, at that time?"*

Oh yeah. I was getting frustrated with myself. I was getting frustrated with the media.

I was looking at our team and saying, "We're too happy."

North Carolina had been in the Final Four the year before and it was halfway through that game when I saw the fire in their eyes.

We were playing like everybody had gotten to the big stage and now we're going to perform.

They were playing to win.

I said, "We are in deep trouble."

And even in the back of my mind I thought, "If we ever get here again, it's going to be different."

What was the difference in mentalities?

- Villanova: Sense of accomplishment
- North Carolina: Hungry to win

If you ask Jay, that's one of his regrets. He let his anxiety create abnormal behavior.

When a team sees the head coach deviate from the norm, it's easy to think the moment is different—it's bigger.

Oregon could relate to this. This was their first Final Four, and Baylor had been there before.

So what I did with the Oregon team was this:

I asked them to fast-forward to their 30-year-old self. (They're between 18-22 years old now.)

If you were 30 and looking back on this experience, what could you regret?

Everybody went around the room and gave one answer. Some of the answers included:

"Not getting enough sleep"
"Get distracted with friends/family traveling in"
"Letting the media/attention take away focus"
"Playing tentatively"

After everyone answered, I asked, "What do all of your answers have in common?"

We all agreed that each answer was in their control. They committed to having no regrets.

Which one was the most common answer?

"Not being what got them there." Essentially not playing to their identity.

That made me think of a concept that seems to help some people get over that feeling.

I asked them to think of a stoplight. What's it like to play yellow? Raise your hand if you know what that feels like.

All their hands shot up.

How would you describe it?

"Second-guessing"
"Playing with doubt"
"Cautious"
"Timid"

That leads to red. What's red?

"Losing your mind"
"Shutting down"

Nick Saban asked earlier, "What breaks you?"

That's red.

So, what's the goal?

To *Play Green*.

What's green?

"All in."

I brought a clip to show them what green looks like in action. It was from one of our discussions earlier in the year. It featured Giannis Antetokounmpo.

It's an incredible example.

Giannis was early in his career and he got the ball stolen at the top of the key. His reaction was instantaneous. He took off sprinting back on defense, ran down the player, and blocked him from behind. Giannis's momentum carried him into the backstop of the hoop as he fell. He immediately got up to make another play.

When he blocked the first shot off the backboard, another player recovered it, and took it in to dunk it.

Giannis met him at the rim and denied him after falling.

Two blocks in less than three seconds. That created a strong visual of what it means to play green.

Each player got a green Sharpie that said *#PlayGreen* on it. They wrote on the tape that contained their words a symbol to help them reset when they could feel themselves going yellow.

If you remember, the team's theme for the postseason was *Rise Above*.

The last video I shared with them was inspired by that theme. It would be the last piece of media they'd see before they played in the Final Four.

The clip featured a runner: Heather Dorniden.

It was the 2008 Big 10 conference championship and Heather was running the 600M final.

Halfway through the race, Heather cut in front of a runner trying to get inside position and was tripped.

She fell.

If you talk with track coaches, 99% of the time, this scenario ends with the athlete pounding their fist and the coach saying, "Get up and finish the race so we can still get our point."

Not with Heather.

She instantaneously got up and regained momentum.

As she picked up steam, she eventually ran down one person. Then another. And right before the finish line she passed the final runner, who happened to be her teammate.

It's nearly impossible for that to happen in such a short race.

Because her reaction was instantaneous and she just did the next right thing, she put herself in the position to overcome what most would consider impossible odds.

As the video finished, there were a lot of moist eyes in the room.

I asked, "What do you admire about that?"

The consensus was how she handled the setback. That was their goal. No matter the setback...*Rise Above*.

THE FINALITY

Oregon lost to the eventual National Champions, Baylor.

For Oregon, the feeling in the game was, "We're going to win. We're going to win. We just lost."

It ended so abruptly. Then we went back into the locker room.

You can tell so much about a team after they lose their last game.

The two phrases I heard the most: "I'm Sorry" and "Thank You."

It was raw.

"I'm Sorry" came from a place where everybody thought they could have done more. Nobody was deflecting or blaming. They were all looking to the inside.

"Thank You" was to the seniors who helped pave the way. (Four seasons ago, they finished 10th in the PAC 12.)

When Kelly Graves, the head coach, walked in to address the team, he said, "There's nothing I can say to make you feel any better. It hurts. And it hurts because it mattered."

From there, all of the coaches hugged each player and thanked them for taking them on an incredible ride.

STAY OR LEAVE
Now, here's what's crazy.

In women's basketball, the draft is within a week of the Final Four.

If you are going to leave early to pursue playing professionally, you have to make that decision within 24 hours.

Sabrina was projected as a potential #1 pick.

Her focus was trying to be all-in with this team. Now that it was over, despite the emotions that surrounded the situation, she needed to make a decision.

We talked at 8:15 the next night (the decision had to be made by 9:00) and Sabrina said she was struggling to make a decision. I asked her to draw a quadrant on a piece of paper.

In the top left quadrant, she wrote down the Pros of Leaving:

> #1 Draft Pick
> Guaranteed Money
> Don't Have To Go To Class
> Better Competition

In the top right quadrant, she wrote down the Cons of Leaving:

> Lifestyle
> Leaving Achievements on the Table

In the bottom left quadrant, she wrote down the Pros of Staying:

Unprecedented Achievement
Relationships with Teammates
Visibility
More Support

In the bottom right quadrant, she wrote down the Cons of Staying:

Injury
Have To Go To Class
Expectations

Here's what the page looked like:

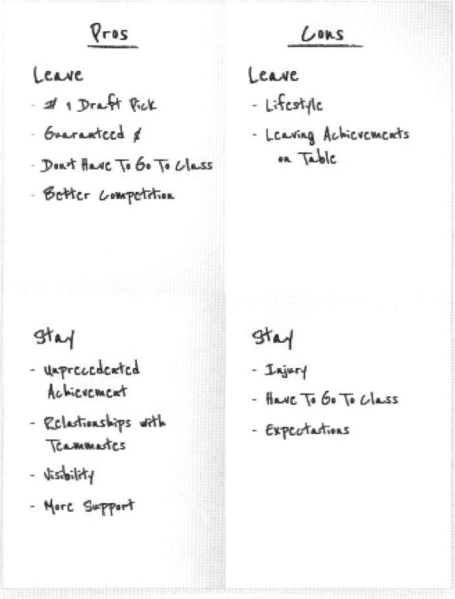

Key point: We wanted to make sure that the opposite of each Con was represented in the Pros column.

Pros

Leave
- # 1 Draft Pick
- Guaranteed $
- Don't Have To Go To Class
- Better Competition

Stay
- Unprecedented Achievement
- Relationships with Teammates
- Visibility
- More Support

Once we did that, we folded the paper in half and only displayed the **Pros**.

Cons breed fear-based emotions and Sabrina didn't want to make a decision based on fear.

Pros breed opportunity-based emotions. That's what she wanted her decision to be fueled by.

Once she had the paper folded in half, she ranked from 1-8 what was most important to her.

Out of confidentiality, I'm not going to share the rankings, but it spit out a decision that was pretty clear.

An hour later this article came out:

THE**PLAYERS'**
TRIBUNE

A Letter to Ducks Nation

Then, Sabrina tweeted this out:

She was going to come back to Eugene, Oregon, for her senior year.

The program will enter next year's preseason polls at #1.

That will bring its own set of unique challenges for Sabrina and the team to *Rise Above*.

From the Author

The *What Drives Winning* TEDx talk was my first attempt at sharing an idea on how to systematize character development. In the talk, I tried to capture the best lesson I learned in the first ten years of my career, when I was working with 5-12th graders at Ledbetter Basketball Academy. The Academy was a developmental environment designed to raise the level of the individual.

I started to ask the question: Can you take character development into the paid-to-win world of athletics? Five years ago, I transitioned from the Academy into becoming a performance consultant and wrote the book *What Drives Winning*. I would ask athletes, "Is your sport moving you closer or further away from the person you want to be?"

I realized through many conversations that sport had the power to take people away from who they wanted to be. I also realized that when you focused on developing the person first, it actually led to better results.

Coaches started to ask, "How do I do this with my team?"

This book was written to help answer that question. The goal: to stimulate thought around how you could introduce some of these concepts in a team setting.

The next few pages offer some ideas on how to create structure, organize content, and find a community of like-minded people.

QUESTIONS TO GET YOU STARTED

1. COMMIT

How often / long do you want to meet?

How could you brand the commitment (think Personal Growth Mondays) so it can be part of your program's identity?

2. PLAN

How would your team answer the two questions at the start of this book? (See page two.)

How could you develop a curriculum based on their answers?

3. FACILITATE

Who is going to facilitate the conversation?

What can the facilitator do to help them find their voice?

4. REINFORCE

What are different ways you can reinforce the message to your team?

How do you personalize the reinforcement?

CHARACTER DEVELOPMENT PLAYBOOK

Building your Character Development Playbook is a proactive approach to get ahead of the human-related issues that could get in the way of the team.

1. COLLECT ASSETS

What's an asset? Assets are videos, articles, pictures, quotes, etc. that are used to facilitate conversations.

2. ORGANIZE YOUR PLAYBOOK

When you see a character skill in action, download it and store it. We have folders that represent each character skill.

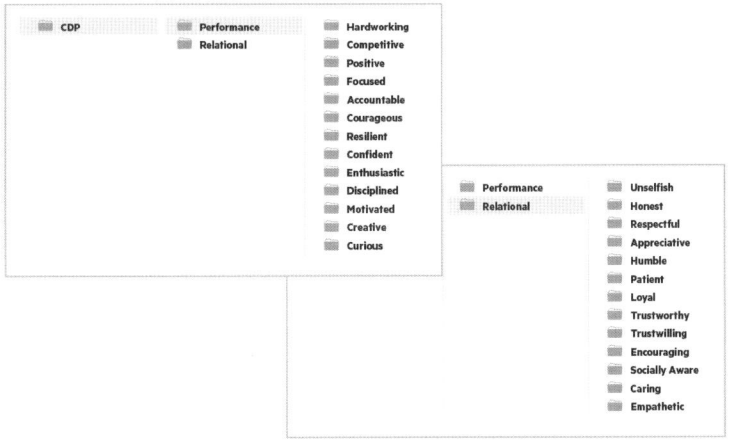

When you collaborate with other leaders it helps you build your asset collection. The What Drives Winning Coaching Lab is a community of coaches that share assets with one another. You can set up your own coaching community or join ours.

For More Information

On how to implement the concepts in this book,
visit Teams.WhatDrivesWinning.com.